C000127996

Natural History

THE GERALD CABLE BOOK AWARD SERIES

Natural History

Craig Beaven

Silverfish Review Press
Eugene, Oregon

Copyright © 2019 by Silverfish Review Press

Cover art: Javanese. Indonesian. Unknown Indonesian. *Burial Mask*. 5th century or earlier. Gold. 7-1/2 x 5-1/4 x 3/4 in. (19.1 x 13.3 x 1.9 cm), The Museum of Fine Arts. Houston. Gift of Alfred C. Glassell, Jr., 2004.2231.

Rodger Moody was the 2017 GCBA final judge.

Except by a reviewer, no part of this book may be reproduced or utilized in any form or by any means, electronic or mechanical, including photocopying and recording, without permission in writing from the publisher.

All Rights Reserved

Published by
Silverfish Review Press
PO Box 3541
Eugene, OR 97403
www.silverfishreviewpress.com

Distributed by
Small Press Distribution
800-869-7553
spd@spdbooks.org
www.spdbooks.org

Library of Congress Cataloging-in-Publication Data

Names: Beaven, Craig, author.
Title: Natural history / by Craig Beaven.
Description: First edition. | Eugene, Oregon : Silverfish Review Press, [2019] | Includes bibliographical references and index.
Identifiers: LCCN 2018053826 | ISBN 9781878851710 (pbk. : alk. paper)
Classification: LCC PS3602.E2639 A6 2019 | DDC 811/.6--dc23
LC record available at https://lccn.loc.gov/2018053826

9 8 7 6 5 4 3 2 First Printing
Printed in the United States of America

CONTENTS

Part V

to Charlie, for the adventure
to Amy, for everything

It was a mystery, although it was right there in a glass case for everybody to see and there was a typewritten card over it telling all about it. But there was something the card couldn't say and what it couldn't say was inside him, a terrible knowledge without any words to it…

—Flannery O'Connor, *Wise Blood*

Natural History

Part I

PRESERVATION

Nothing can be spared
from time, just don't tell

our donors. Here in the museum
it seems human endeavor

is winning—the finest invisible
non-reflective glass

allows *Lama Deity*
to be in this room, and in

its own room, where breath
can't touch it. Pre-Elamite, we hold it

in Texas, shoot it for the archives.
It makes sense

that all our donors
have the age

cut from their faces, hair sewn
onto their hair, breasts dialed back

40 years or more. A museum
is a monument

to death aversion. As the hurricane
approached—still 12 hours away, still

hot and sunny
in our part of the sky—we went out

with all our neighbors
to photograph our houses

for insurance.
Roof torn away tonight, tree

through a window, you will need proof
that yesterday things existed

intact. My neighbor
who's done this many times

walks me through it.
We tied our lawn furniture

to a tree, brought all our plants inside. Before
and after. Signs, under the sill,

of horizontal rain damage.
Taking the pictures, you have to imagine

what will be destroyed, and how.
You shoot your car

in the driveway, the tree
over your car. Inside—spines

of books, stacks of records.
I open my closet door

and try to get all the shirts
in the frame. These are my clothes,

this is my stuff. If everything in this photo
is gone tomorrow

I want everything here
given back.

LATE SHIFT IN THE CHILDREN'S SECTION

After everyone has gone and the kids
have had their way with the stacks
I come in like a reverse patron
and restore the jangled alphabet
for tomorrow's eagerness: dinosaurs,
mummies, the customs of Native Americans;

how long until the Hemingway biography
for children, how many nights until
I discovered it there at the top, beside
Pasteur, Sacajawea, Alfred Morse,
and how can Hemingway die
in a biography written for kids:

He was holding his favorite rifle,
there was a brilliant flash of light,
and Hemingway was dead.

Held it close, then—a pulse
like lightning? Dawn bursts
just over the sill? Who
was reassured
by this version? No
trips to the clinics,
no earlier attempts. He only bullfights, he only big game
hunts, works eight hours a day on sentences
and it causes no problems whatsoever.

Why, at that point in my life, had I read
every Hemingway bio for grown-ups,
that obsess his death, and his father's; biographers
close reading all the prose
and finding it's a single, long confession.
One book wants to examine it

as closely as possible, one ends
with a magic trick. In children's stories
every boy is heroic, every lost child
restored at the end, confusions resolved
like waking from a bad dream.
Before I could enter my section I had to wait

for it to close, and I watched the fathers,
imagined myself older, sleepy
the way they seemed, imagined
I would have children of my own
and the father I would be,
and if I could have a child, but I can't,
and if I could have a child, what would I tell him
if he asked about suicide, as surely he would,
since everyone learns about it
eventually, how do you keep them from the world
even as they must live in it—Listen: it isn't light
or mysterious or beautiful,
a person becomes
so sad and lost
they think they can't stand another day,
but there's no such thing
as no chance for survival,
you'll never be alone
as long as you're with me.

WE ARE HAPPY

1

Whatever of us that is in this wand—
the invisible code of our lives—
whatever is contained there
will not make it to the children
we have. Whatever our children take
they will take through proximity,
a lifetime close together, car trips, meals, fathers especially
must remove their shirts
and hold a newborn
right against your chest, and speak to them,
and look them in the eye. This creates attachment—
stronger, healthier immune system, gain weight
more quickly, but no one knows why,
we are happy.

2

Our eggs are downtown under safety lights
dividing at 3 a.m. Technicians chart their growth
and will call when they're ready, I'll call my boss,
Not feeling
well today. Exit interstate
to our possible future
children, now moved
from their wet dishes
to a long wand—
they have photographed
them—our cells—to hang
on the fridge, healthy ones like a cluster
of soap bubbles, the other
more angular, stony, a shard of safety glass plucked

from a car seat with tweezers,
we are happy.

3

Picture in your mind a pool of still water.
Recall your fondest memories.
No exercise, no stress. See, in your mind, the still
dark water. The eggs
are attaching, sinking roots down
in the lining

in your body, a lining we created
with injections. See
the water, untroubled, unclouded.
At the bottom: a sphere
like a cotton ball
rests on the dark floor.
Becomes fixed. Begins to grow.

4

They go in through your navel, we are happy.
They go in with a scope and if, on the monitor,
the light inside shows raised lines
like a whelp, contours like a mountain range,
they'll go back in with a laser
and burn them off.
Nice shower cap. Nice booties.
No one knows how the ridges inside you
grew there, or how they prevent eggs
from attaching. You sleep and wake
ten times in ten minutes, each time asking *did you get
breakfast, did you wait long, why is it
so cold in here?* We are happy.

5

Nexus of all things—intersection
of 4 a.m. and cloud cover, storm system
and don't ejaculate for three days,
in the crosshairs of
this movie, this cup, the timing,
eggs coming down the long tubes,
safe lights
and a needle. I brought a book
to pass the wait, handed my sample
through a window, centrifuge on the counter
becomes part
of the body's process.
The confluence of all things together:
our work schedules allowing a day off,
all things must converge
in this petri dish, technician
in surgical mask—one small breath
could disrupt the whole thing—in retrospect: why
did we ever believe?
We are happy.

6

Waiting in one room to see
how they mispronounce our name today:
Beaver. Beeven. It's like heaven
with a B, we tell each nurse, like heaven
with a B. The blood bubbles red
so dark it seems black—where do they take it—
your blood, my *contribution*, wait in one chamber,
summoned to the next, but there are so many doors
we can't go through. We'll call you. At work
you close your office door,
your estrogen levels are safe, but it was just
your blood, no one else's, no one there

inside you, their body
unspooling into life.

7

I admit that I'm skeptical—*Black Dreams*—
that this is where our child begins, coiled
in this moment: Do not use soap, lubricants, or saliva. Make sure
it all goes in the cup. They're on a piano bench, it takes him
forever. I close my eyes, hold the cup close, a feeling
that lasts as long as a sneeze. Was this the moment
where our daughter begins? Please wash your hands
and return the movie to its case, someone
tries the door—*just a minute*—
close the tv in its cabinet. Restore this room
to the order you found it. No one
was here. This room has never been used before.

8

In the event of the death of the male partner,
we are happy,
in the event of the death of the last surviving partner,
we are happy,
I choose to have the eggs
destroyed / donated / saved to be reused by me.
You could die
and I could have our child with another woman.
We could divorce
and you could have our child on your own. If we both die
someone can have our child
ten years from now, ejecting the metal cylinder
from its chamber, so cold it steams, someone
in a gown, waiting in the next room.
We hereby swear to have read this document on this day
and we are happy.

9

Three paths into your body,

we are happy,

scope, laser, long needle,

we are happy,

three injections

each night before sleep,

we are happy,

syringes go in the safety box

beneath the bed, we are happy,

still there a year later, we are happy.

10

I lay my hand against your stomach,
a glass of water,
small pebble
at the bottom. The glass

in a dark room, lit
by an open door in the distance.
The pebble at the bottom
begins to dissolve, breaks
into cloud
that takes a new shape

like sediment in a current

like a flock of birds lifting. This is how
I picture the process
although all tests tell me
none of it was true:
no pebble, no glass of water, and certainly
no new shape forming.

But there was a door,
a white rectangle
in the distance.
That part was real.

UNPACKING THE STONE BUDDHA

Like all weaklings, I desire
something else—
intangible, but shaded and cool,
just on the other side
of this high, stone wall, the loose clear chime
of ice in glasses, and someone diving
into a pool. It's only Wednesday afternoon
but there's a little garden party, tuxedoed men
with silver trays, quiet laughter, you catch glimpses
through the hedges, or ivy-covered
iron bars. They have a shaded grass median
to jog through. There is a quiet intersection
with stone gazebo and fountain.
You can turn the corner
and relax in the sculpture garden
among ancient masterpieces, among modern works
few people understand.
Across the street, in the Museum of Fine Art,
they're unpacking the stone Buddha
from its wooden crate. At 11 a.m. it's 99 degrees
and 80% humidity. The lawn crews throughout the city
seem unfazed. In the basement, unseen
by Houston's millions, they unpack the stone Buddha
on loan from Ho Chi Minh City. Sandstone,
2,000 years old, removed from the earth in 1863, buried there,
they believe, by flood. No one knows
about this, no one comes to see it
three months on display—a basement gallery
where no sun can touch it, dimmed lights
and dark painted walls most guests mistake
as closed.
I leave my office with headaches
from the cold air we're piping in
and walk the rich neighborhood.

By living here, they can keep everything at bay—even seasons:
when the flowers stop blooming
they're dug out. With money, they have conquered
landscape, the drab moments
between color. In the basement, the stone Buddha.
Cut from the rock, polished down to these
thin fingers, one foot raised as if about to step down
from the 2x4's surrounding it, into a strange kind
of afterlife. Down in this dark room
we're trying to bury it like the river, to put it back
where it belongs. We're holding our breath
with a crowbar, popping each board.
It can only be lifted out by hand;
we must touch it, although the contract says
no one can touch it. I go look at it,
squinting through the dark.
When our three months expire
we send it back.

GHAZAL

These hands will never grow as large as my father's.
The teacher said: all young poets must read their fathers.

In the story, two crows fly north until
their bodies turn blue. The end is the whispering of a father.

Some autumn we rode bikes through the country.
At dusk he kept on; breathless, I could go no farther.

Blessing at each meal: left hand on your stomach,
right hand touches forehead, begin: *In the name of the Father.*

They share a name: the old man lying in bed
and the narrow clock in the hall: *Grandfather.*

After the funeral, we had no reason to return to the town.
Change plate, saltshaker, a shot glass: all that remain of a father.

2

In the smelting plant, iron dust swirls the air
like flies, pointillism of a thousand dancing figures:

the foreman's office, rejected from Louisville's best factory job
because the curve of his spine, my eighteen-year-old father

goes back to the bus, rocking home
through snow and drizzle, 8 a.m. on a Monday:

Mom still in bed, my older sister awake
in her crib, and he leans to her, says the word *father,*

to hear it, make it real.
As kids we were amazed

by his exhaustion, how he could sleep on the couch,
even as the house raged. Is *rage* another name for *father*?

More like *passion*, a father's desire to hold
the things he loves, a love too great to be rational.

3

My childhood insomnia cure was recite every prayer
I knew. Nights stumbling to sleep over the *Our Father*.

She argues with my quiet. I say
I'm helpless: *It's something I got from my father*.

Imagine Christmas morning, a brightly colored package,
trying it on in front of the mirror.

My build, my body, the bones in my face;
before it was all mine, it was my father's.

They say a love poem is locked in a chest
at the bottom of the sea. I say: a father.

And this too, is true: I never heard my first name
until I started school. *Richard?*

the teacher called, *Richard?*
The name of my father.

Part II

A CURRENT ATLAS OF THE COMMONWEALTH OF VIRGINIA

The statues are no longer fragments—we are

Essex, Southampton, New London, Wales.
Lining all that blue of ocean: King and Queen
County, city of Westminster, city of Suffolk.
Vein of I-95: exits

where the sniper killed. The home
of Patrick Henry. Dismal Swamp tours
in a glass-bottomed boat. You can feel
the bullet holes in the walls

of Appomattox Courthouse.
The capitol roses were brought over
from England. The rain that feeds them
has no name or border. Every battle

has been noted and marked
but when you pull over
to the shoulder
the inscription on the pillar
tells you very little
about the forest you're looking at.

Proposition 97A before the council: refortify the trenches
at Cold Harbor, or leave them
as the soldiers left them,
and let them erode. Dugouts
once six feet deep
but time
is filling them in.

The vote is 8-1 for a certain
type of memory, therefore:
blue dawn, men on their bellies
in the autumn chill
digging trenches in a Civil War battlefield.

IN THE MUSEUM OF PERSONAL HISTORY

There are two museums. In one

I walk among crucifixions, pietas, adoration
of the magi. The second museum
is identical: every object in the collection
photographed to a hard drive, shot
front and back, close-up
of signature, detail of any cracks
or visible brushstrokes. One museum is
two city blocks, four stories, gift shop and café; the other
fits in a black box
the size of a small suitcase, searchable
by a thousand different key words. In one museum
I call up
Javanese Burial Mask, 400 A.D., gold
thin as onion skin, fine cuts for eyelashes
and brows. Someone hammered it out
on the day of burial. Someone
laid it on a corpse; when it cracked
years later someone mended it.
Glows on my monitor a few seconds.
It made you more presentable to the gods
of the afterlife. I approve and click *next*.

Will you take our picture?

When the real museum is closed
and the windows are dark
our photographer comes in
to record what it looks like—

Will you take our picture?

Hold still. Mission San Juan, Mission
Concepción, Amy pulls her hair back
and people we don't know dodge

the frame. Colonial-era Spanish
settlements. A bible from 1408.
A chalice, a crucifix.
This is how they pumped water
from the depths beneath the desert.

A wind comes up so Amy pulls her hair back—
one more says the guy holding our camera.
We ate downtown by the river, you were trying
to get virgin daiquiris but the waiter
misheard, or the bartender couldn't abstain,
one sip and send it back. It was the first time
we had placed a syringe in the refrigerator
for a month, waiting
for the calendar to indicate
the day. You said the drug burned
its cold inside you. It seemed too easy—alcohol pads,
needle and plunger, the liquid's startled dance
before compressing. In the real museum

I walk through the Byzantine period,
Jesus upon Jesus, *Madonna and Child with Souls,*
How many renderings of the crucifixion
will be enough? I had to raise $400,000
so the museum could get this one. Thank you, Oil & Gas Company,
your name will forever be on the wall
beside Jesus' feet, where Mary Magdalene kneels
weeping. *St. Veronica's Veil, Journey to Nazareth,*
Study for Annunciation.

Hold still. Amy wants one without her glasses,
she wore glasses for years but there is no record
although in some you can see light reflecting
from the invisible lenses in her hands.

This door, c. 1690. It lasted long enough
to become
a relic, long enough

for the state to preserve it, and now us.

This is another museum, the one
of our lives, putting it all together
in photo albums
like we're trying to prove something,
like an argument no one else is having.

Hold still, Jesus. No photographs
of Calvary, we have to invent
the weather that day, which was gold leaf, invent
his body—skeletal, nimbus—decide
how the nails went in. Grass emerald

and spiky. Hills receding to distance—will the blood
run or gush? The blood
is flaking, *Hold still*
and I push the needle in
below your navel, it seems too long, too heavy,
vial of cold hormones
to send eggs down, or indicate to eggs
they should attach now,
or divide. I try to locate the moment
of conception in this. Hold still, we say, indiscriminately,
out loud, hold still, just this once, please.

BRAIDS

I believed in seeing a painting
in person, after years
of reproductions. Was I "passionate"
or just naïve? In *Braids*
nothing happens. In Wyeth's *Braids*
there is only
each piece of hair, known intimately by God
and the painter, strand and strand
brought in
to hold its own turning. High school art history
and it beats across the screen, mote-mottled,
projection-warped—years later I drove
three days
to stand here. This
is where he stood, arm's length
from the canvas. This
is Maine at the end of April; tomorrow
it snows, and we watch an old man
march into the ocean, submerge himself,
walk out and shake it off.
Why, standing at *Braids,* can I think
not of this painting, but of approaching
Press 40, the day
after graduating high school,
and what conspires to make the plant foreman
start me at Press 40, of 44 presses?
What does Wyeth
have to do with graveyard shift
making dashboards
except for fathers
and concentration? The guy at 39 has sleeves
of scar tissue, a purple luminescence
poorly stitched on. Number 40
is the largest machine in the state. I know

because my father built it.
It slows my work to realize: have I seen this
before, in dream? Drafting table, white lines
on blue paper, the ghost of it emerging
with each revision. He brought me here as a kid
to explain how it worked,
describe the tonnage, the many men
it took. My father who was, at that moment,
asleep, who I would pass in the kitchen
this morning, on my way to bed, on his way
here, to see how I did
and if they need anything—
replacement parts or adjustments. So I came
to the far edge of a continent, so
I walked through the field
from *Christina's World*—
Why save any of this
from the fire? Dear Origin Myth, are you
in art history class
or night shift hours
sanding the rough edges of dashboards? I was there
as a way of apologizing,
but no one heard it
amid the din,
no one noticed such a gesture
in the filing away of excess plastic. In *Braids*
she stands alone in a cold,
dark room, looking away.
Someone is calling
but it doesn't break her spell.
They've been calling forever
but they don't know her name.
The house is empty and quiet.
This is the story of your life.

TALKING IT OUT BEFORE CATEGORY 4

In a city without winter
the leaves don't change-and-fall,
they merely fall, without fanfare,
without meaning. I was afraid

to move here, where we knew
none of the 4 million, and had
no place to stay. The storm

is just off the coast
40 miles away. It is passing across the beach
and the live oak
in our yard
is trying to come undone. In school

I was afraid of school. Living downtown
I was afraid of downtown. My doctor said
anxiety is only allowable

if you're really in danger. In a minute
the storm blows the power out
but we all live through this, everyone
who came to my house for shelter.
The walls visibly shake.
It goes right over our home,
the eye of it. In a city without winter

there is a threat
of these storms. My doctor said
anxiety is only allowable
if you're *really* in danger, i.e. someone
is holding a gun to your head, then
you can worry, but driving to work
in no traffic, on a clear day?

Here, in the dark
and rain, the live oak twists and thrashes
as if struggling to be free
of its own form. What's wrong?
It's strange: no amount of prescriptions
and no amount of dosage
and no amount of truth
can touch me.

SELF-PORTRAIT WITH ORTHO TRI-CYCLEN

We believed it was your pills
that kept our lives in order—little dial,
little clock face.

We lived inside something
as hot as fire. The pill was us

being responsible: young, unmarried, we woke
and candles along the mantle

were melted
without ever being lit, white wick there
in the hardened puddle.
We believed in the pills
like they were money

or autumn, things that,
when arrived, would set
everything right.

I don't feel stupid
looking back, believing in a pill, our plans

in the dot on your tongue,
then gone. *One day*, if someone asked, *sure*,
but now we're young and poor
and in school, live meagerly. I don't feel

stupid, *Don't forget
your pill*, it means
so much to us. It meant nothing.

I think in Lexington your pendant still hangs
on the doorknob where we left it
12 years ago, tiny face of your grandmother

clasped there in the dark, as the chain tarnishes.

This is a strange way to write about death.
It's a strange way to remember your youth:
to have been wrong about something
you relied on
above all else.

Should we feel differently now
about the act of making, now that we know,

together, we do not make?
We do this. We love it. It won't have
that outcome, but others,
countless others.

WE ARE HAPPY

If you arrive early enough
to your office downtown
you can hear the lion
wake, roar from his cave, declare dominion
over whatever lies beyond
the moat that holds him in,
and all of Houston's grackles
burst from the trees—they've never
had legions eaten
by lion, but instinct
tells them what to fear.
The lion wants badly
to hunt, and when they slip
raw steaks through the drawer
he creeps off
behind the rock, stalks between
two trees, and pounces. *My brother died in utero*
is a way of saying *miscarriage*,
I was eight years old, my dad
took us to get a Christmas tree
and we ate fast food
three nights in a row. My mother was in bed
alone, and I was told
not to grieve, one of those times
someone pulls you close to the couch,
turns the TV down low, puts their face
right at your level, and looks serious and confused,
and tells you something important
that you don't understand.

Part III

WE WILL NEVER FORGET

What we remember most
was never real:
there was never a white van
but we feared it. Yes, he was
shooting, but no van, and
it wasn't white, why
did we say otherwise?
You had to factor it
in, avoid places
by the interstate
within eyesight.
We had stopped
at that exit
before; he used the pay phone
right by our house.
There was no
white van rolling slowly
down our street; we got up
and went inside. We couldn't
go jogging. Everything
suddenly different: school
cancelled—wouldn't a group
of children, walking in line
be perfect? He had never
been downtown so we went
to the park in the river,
police there, someone had seen
the van on the hill, a good
spot for it. We went
to the diner that resembled
a diner from the 50's, or from
a movie about the 50's:
on the television
helicopter spins above

white van, back road
past Rappahannock,
the helicopter is saying
pull over and cops swarm,
but he's a house painter,
it turned out there wasn't
a white van, so why
did we invent one? What did it do
for us? Gas stations hung blue tarps
like curtains
so no one could see you
standing there. Part of history
now, the imaginary
white van more known
than the real gray sedan.
When we've died
and this is a historic site
how will they erect the marker?
When we remember these days
with diorama
what will they include
as prop? Put a tree
standing in for death.
Tilt the whole scene
to the dark. Make each leaf
from a shard of stained glass.
Put a man speaking
to an officer, a man
who wants to be part
of it, pushes
his fingers through his hair.
A man remembering
clearly, saying yes
I am sure, and an officer there
taking down in a pad
every word.

ELEGY

Told that we could not make another
I looked out from the 17th floor, oil platforms in a line

on the water, worried not for myself
but for my family, grieved something called a *line*,

thread
running through names, binding

us together. Some friends won't have children
because of their line—

addiction in there, a suicide, they choose
to be the last of the line,

protecting the child they are refusing;
I guess they love them, the way I loved children ·

I couldn't make. I never worried. The science
is so simple, even children

are taught how it happens. I thought of blood
as a glass case, holding relics of a tribe,

the way our face appears
in the earliest known photograph

of a Beaven, same eyes and nose—
take whatever bones

you need, reach in for a cupful of blood
to divide inside you. They kept pulling our blood,

tied off like a junkie, placed blood
against light to see.

The body is a temple:
I enter the sacristy and light a candle. The body

begins as line—filament
unloosening. Blood is the string

holding everything together,
everything but you and me.

IN THE CONSERVATION ROOM

I

History's subconscious: we descend
the hidden elevator only our plastic badges
operate. The Artax shoots an x-ray
of Rembrandt's *Portrait*. Climate controlled,
light controlled, breath held back
with surgical mask. Hard to raise funds
for what no one ever sees. They want to give
to the big installation, room-sized
mural, not behind the scenes, not
chemical. We have to make donors
feel like Medicis—to preserve this
Rembrandt is *the responsibility of*
great patrons throughout time, and
our part for future generations,
if any future people come
to the museum, and if they feel
something other than derision
when they gaze at her.
Without fail, everyone says *She's ugly.*
The value is the signature in the corner,
and her eyes look real, and he put in
the light reflecting on her earrings.
I bring all out of town guests
to look at it. There are 52 Rembrandts
in the U.S. Here we assign it a barcode,
no longer art, just a series of chemical
compounds, series of problems. No
object is beyond repair. How many
have performed this ritual on this
woman—eyepiece, mouth covered with cloth,
slow scanning every inch of face
and hair? We lean in as close as we can

like a prayer mat we whisper to, like
a plate of water we would drink from.
Cotton gloves and canned air, to pass it on
we cannot touch it.

2

                    To pass it on
we cannot touch it—bone and blood,
invisible code thinner
than a human hair, they contained it
in a long wand, photographed
with microscope, enlarged
to the size of a baseball. In this room
there are no lights, just
lie down, wait fifteen minutes,
a nurse pokes her head in to say
you can get dressed now.
To pass on this gossamer nothing
they had to invent the device
that could hold it, they had to
discover what it was,
photograph it
to prove its existence. Ghost, wind, fog there
and then gone in sunlight, a single flake
of Houston snow: it can get as close
as the eaves of the house
but no further, vanishes
in the earth's warmth, we reach up
our arms but can't touch it.

3

Dear Rorschach Test that would reveal
our lives to us, dear never even a ghost, never enough
of you to die, pattern of black ink
on plain copy paper, I am making you
into an ekphrastic poem. I made you real
in my mind for years. When I speak
I'm speaking to fantasy, speculation. I wanted
to name you Richard after my father, I
began to believe, was told that to believe
was better, that a positive mind
could make things happen, things
that could never happen. As close as you came
was ink-jet dots on paper, *blastocyst*,
genetic material condensed, separated
and centrifuged. *Portrait of Non-Man.*
I craved you, non-you, gazing intently each day,
staring as if at a masterpiece handed down
400 years; you were us, ink-blots on paper,
you were our history, our blood, you held all of us
in your coils. You were nothing.
We couldn't save you.

A PINT OF BIG TWO-HEARTED

My friend loves this beer
and doesn't know anything
about Hemingway or black crickets
or the swamp we must enter
but not today—she tastes it without
Nick Adams making flapjacks
over an open fire, or Vonnegut's essay
detailing his own obsession.
She doesn't know
the Big Two-Hearted is a river
that seems inaccessible on maps.
I've been as far north as Petoskey in February.
crystal cold and deserted, you could walk
the rows of pines and feel
America was lost and never
coming back. I learned to love this beer
at a bar in Ann Arbor; it's bitter
and cold and red bordering on black
or purple depending on the light.
We played *Black Love* on the jukebox.
We had no where to live, and no where
to be. My friend loves this beer and asks
at every bar, but she's never read
Hemingway's letters, even as an old man
railing against his parents, their disapproval.
She doesn't know his son's names, or
their fates. Do I enjoy a pint
more than she, because Hadley
left the valise on the train and there are stories
we're never going to get? I've been as far as Petoskey
deserted in winter, a diner open, a bad
Italian place, a Catholic church no one
went to. All the homes on the lake
boarded up for winter, all the waves on the lake

frozen over, kids drive out on the water
to get away, to get further away from everything.
I have a magnet from the gift shop
at Hemingway's childhood home, I'm not sure why;
it's like drinking a pint
of Big Two-Hearted. You can't go in
the birthplace—someone lives there,
but the childhood home is being restored. They had the parlor
stripped back to the original wallpaper. When we went
it was snowing
in mid-October, famous snow:
it was the earliest it had ever snowed
in the recorded history of that town. No matter
how amazing, how unprecedented
and phenomenal, the snow
was all gone by afternoon
and never coming back.

ODE: TO THE PEOPLE WHO DRIVE BY
AND SHOUT INSULTS WHILE I'M JOGGING

The need to diminish others, without
knowing why, without time to even consider: *hey*

hot stuff, which means
I'm cold nothing, which means to jog
is an idea of becoming more attractive,
a car of teenagers feels compelled
to let me know it isn't working.

Looking good, which means looking bad,
red-faced in the heat, stoop-shouldered
as if wilting, as if mid-collapse. Often
just a wolf-whistle, an exaggerated
woo-hoo, I look up
and see laughing speeding away, they're delighted

to pull me from my asphalt
reverie, cloud reverie, waterfowl
meditation. Heron or egret and the long
lift off down the bayou, *Put a shirt on.*
It's hard to stay focused, daily, on God.

It's hard to forget
that you're running, which is the only way
to do it: ignore
the two and a half miles
to the interstate, the two and a half miles back.

Although at dusk
the bats swim so close
I hear the ticking of their jaws,
I don't fear them, my body echoes back
too large to be food. Erratic swirl, black on black,
they scream and listen. There is nothing
that can't be taken away.

Sweet hecklers, don't they know
all of us are in it together, all of us
are being gathered, waiting
to take our place
on that dark boat,
the one that bears us away
and never returns.
The dark is final, once and for all.

Faster fatty, faster. I too have suffered. I too
have perished here along the shore. Don't stop
at shouts and scorn; take a cupful of sand
and bury my corpse
along this river. May you be safe
and may this harmless storm
exhaust its rage soon enough.

Pause. Give three cupfuls of sand.
And go on your way.

Part IV

CASE ASSESSMENT

Though he works and worries, the farmer
never reaches down to where the seed turns
to summer

We are trying to decide

    if this is our son

        growing six months

in the body of

    last name blacked

        for privacy we

go over paper

    work on lunch meet in

        the sculpture garden has

taken the Rodin

    to storage Monday we have 48 hours

        to decide you can't keep

everyone waiting

    the hundred other

        couples who might

become his

    parents she is

        18 hobbies cooking dancing

I wanted the father there all

        his information

                in case my son

ever asks and so we'll know

        how to decide

                I wanted more

time the document begins

        to blur handwritten

                photocopied faxed

another artifact

        in the collection

                ink on paper

sonogram cloud

        in the box

                beneath the bed

which one day he will open

        and put himself together

SAINTHOOD

1

Winter, and the flower has bloomed white
at the tip top of the bush

like a child's ball caught high
in the branches.

City lights too much
for stars. Leaf drip

like a second rain.
I walked out today and a few wrens—
that white stripe
over the oil drop eye.
Moon fraction
shimmered on low
at the end of the street. The flower

is never still, opens out to begin
folding back, browns and softens,
a constant turning.

This far south
winter
is just a long autumn
weakening to spring.

2

In the story I'm writing Casey comes back—
back to his name, back to the booth
at the diner, the couch
in his dad's basement. Between

leaving and returning

were Latin vespers, stones
to be knelt on. The only town left
is the one we grew up in.

3

The skeleton dreams of sinew, never
of bone. The way a rake left out in the sun
burns a rake shadow in the grass.

Put your body through the tiredness
and stay awake all night. Kneel
on the stone and on the stone
is chipped glass. The closest
we can get without dying:
the wounds of the cross
opening. CAT scan and theory
that our mind,
with enough focus and concentration,
rips the skin
of hands and feet—
meant to disprove, but
how is that not divine,
thought attending
one spot, forcing a hole
in the palm
where no nail was?

4

Really, I'm not sure how you become
a saint. Most have visions, or
suffer greatly, or both.

Ordained, his name was changed:
Brother Pio Mary of the Holy Eucharist—
his body became the body
of she whose body
was the body of bread
which is the body—

kneeling before the blue
plaster robes
of Mary, girl-faced Mary.
The small click of the rosary.
A dark
centuries old and long.

5

It's commonly understood
that the problem with stigmata
is ego and desire—a blood
trophy, bragging. It feels like fire
at the opening, and prevents
sleep. Anyway, he never
got it—prayed and stayed prostrate
for a long time, and suffered,
and was silent, but none of it
led to opening. He was an artist,
sent me a pencil drawing
from the friary, stag
with candelabra for antlers
and ghost in the forest
lighting the candles with a long taper.
We were altar boys together at his dad's
remarriage. When he left the order
and reentered life
his first job was at a glass factory
driving a fork-lift, moving towers
of sheets of clear glass, and standing

at the line where they come off
the press, all that sand
burned to invisibility, there were
unlimited cotton gloves
but carrying the sheets over
he got cut anyway, right on the palm
where he had prayed for so long.
He made more money than I ever have.
They did his dispensation over the phone
in Latin, at the job site, as he had no phone
in the room he rented. He said after 10 hour
shifts you thought everywhere
were glass columns, and you tread
so carefully among them,
he said I could be carrying some right now
and not know it, except the air
in my hands
would be much heavier.

RECURRING DREAM OF THE MUSEUM

I

We can't display the entire
collection at once; 20 miles away
in an industrial warehouse
storage has more paintings
than the real museum, better
security and climate controls.
Was the jade hand beautiful

all those years packed away? Here
it seems blurry—
pure light and not
stone. Seems to move like a sea—
the same deep
blue-green. Doesn't appear to be
heavy, chipped once
on the smallest finger
as it lasted two thousand years.
In storage
a century because
it couldn't clear customs—
Guatemala said it was taken
on false pretense and belongs
there, and we said
you can't display it right
and no one would see it.

In the warehouse
the pictures are being *rested*—
every painting blank
under protective black cloth.
All those masterpieces
in the dark; a museum
no one can visit.

65

2

The first museum ever made
was a way of praying. Household
cabinet or shelf, arranging objects
of your dead. You lit
a bowl of oil. Spoke aloud
to someone who wasn't there.
You hoped the display
pleased them enough
they would bless you from wherever they are.
The world was old
even then, already
every object crumbled
in our hands.

3

When I allowed myself
an image of the future, I thought
I would name a son James—
part of my father's name—
but in adoption
it's not right
to extend a line that way.
And it's no big deal to me
now, and maybe never was, but
it is a fact of how
my son was born. Is the jade hand
meaningful, or are we just
writing a story? What would it be
without our presentation—
"invisible" wire floats it
mid-air, and the pedestal
illuminates up and through.
Today, rifling through my nightstand,

I found a parking pass
for Acadia National Forest
from 16 years ago. Out past the suburbs
a lake has at last dried up
revealing chunks of space shuttle debris—
on display soon
at the public library. In the museum

when it's time to show
Afghani Burial Jewels
we examine
excavation photos, put out
on a table covered in fine black cloth
73 golden tears
in the shape of a child. She died
and turned to dust
and even the dust disappeared
but the golden shape of her remains.

ROSE GARDEN PAGODA

This rose is a labyrinth, its turning
a kind of Zen garden
you follow
to an empty center.
This is why cathedrals
were invented—the tall windows
let the light in
and the light moves
as the church turns on the turning
earth. The dream of a perfect room.
In the room is the sacristy, on
the altar, on a cloth blessed
with a sprinkle of holy water
and incense clouds, both
from a brass scepter. In the gold foil
sacristy, locked, is a small white disc—
miracle of grass turned golden,
threshed, baked and pressed
with a cross. You eat it, your mouth the next
chamber. And the air a miracle, and the dust
trapped in sun's streaming.
Small white disc like a pretend coin,
symbolic, symbol box in a symbol room
and a symbol song
and you cross yourself, bless yourself,
affirm these gestures and motions
involve God.

WHERE AMY WORKS

Sit on a bench downtown and wait
for it—silent ambulance stops under
the portico, a small
red plastic cooler
with a heart inside, or a kidney,
all manner of body comes here
packed in the everyday ice
you'd put in a drink. He doesn't
act differently—hold it outstretched
as if offering to the gods. So light
it must feel empty. Will says
today we got a human hand.

One day you turn the corner
to a crate of baby pigs
wheeled down the hall. One day
you share the elevator
with a lab-coated man
cradling a baby chimp,
shushing it, plunger protruding
from the leathery chest, needle
deep in there
piercing the heart.

Part V

AT THE MUSEUM OF FUNERAL HISTORY

In the back, encased in glass,
on a pedestal, enshrined: the original filament

from JFK's eternal flame:
thin wire heated by electric,

gas breath sighs over, igniting,
just a coat hanger or piece of trash, filament

from his original fire. A strand of genes
is a filament,

holding your blood's
code, the element

that will form
your bones. How many wept at this fire?

Who came to pour their lament—
and then it began to falter, new element

installed, this one boxed up,
sealed in its own coffin,

we no longer even know
what these elements

help us remember: They have the programs
from Lincoln's funeral—small element

of history; they have the bill of sale
for McKinley's embalming, fiber

weave paper burning yellow at the edges.
A new two-inch wire filament

burning at Kennedy's grave,
surviving the elements,

wind ruffles its glow, snow melts in a circle, rain
cannot douse its light. You must know

by now what I'm talking about.
You must know what I mean by filament,

element, strand of DNA. In one there is a thin wire flame
at a grave in Virginia. The other heats up

inside a bulb, and the bulb—frosted—emits light.
In one it is all the elements

that make a body. In another, it is all the elements
that do not.

STARGAZER'S FIELD

Days before you were born
I walked to the top of the mountain.
There were further, higher peaks, and snow
falling on them, white
filling in between
black pines. The sky
seemed closer than the earth.
I thought of the distance between you and I
and how I would bridge that distance.
At the top of the mountain
they raised sheep and rams, in separate pens,
a thin line of wire
between them. I knew that thin line—
if you were to touch it
it would warm your hands,
you would feel it in your bones, and although
the rams wanted to cross
they had learned not to.
They stood perfectly still in the snow, occasionally
dipping for a mouthful of grass.
People have been walking up the mountain
for thousands of years, to look out
at the bowl of mountains. South
beyond the valley, as land slopes
to the sea, you were waiting across a continent just days
to be born. I thought of you
safe in your dark water, and thought of you
in ten years. We will walk up here together
to look at the rams, to look out
into the valley. We will see mountains,
and as clouds move, further mountains
like a curtain pulling back across a stage.
We will hear the report of rifle shot.
We will wear orange vests that say
don't shoot, I'm human.

THE LAST CONFEDERATE TREE TELLS ALL

Cannons along the roadside
hold the last line of fortification
from 140 years ago. They seem

even more ancient, as if pulled
from depths of the sea; smaller after a century
of rain, moss covered. You can climb up

and have your picture taken,
follow their line of aim—traffic,
a stoplight, the condo's fourth floor.

Right now, in Richmond, Virginia,
The Last Confederate Tree is waiting
for the speech we will inscribe on it, balanced

on sawhorses, barkskin shucked
aside, where the knife is poised—
the tree meant nothing for years, but then

it kept on living,
even as the world it was born in
died slowly, still, it was only a tree

until a hurricane felled it. The tree
from all the watercolors
of the White House of the Confederacy, shorter then,

barely shading the portico door,
and leafless in photos
of the Davis family: severe in their starched,

dark finery; eyes painted-on after they shut them
to afternoon's light, the sky
spider-veined, cracking

over downtown. The tree, they have decided,
will be cut into pieces—presented to the Sons
and Daughters—each small piece

set with an inscription,
and one held behind glass
in the museum with other relics—chain

from a lost anchor,
shirt with its original bloodstain,
and the maps of this place

that have faded more slowly
than the land they're of.
The cannons remain vigilant

against everyone leaving the video store. Already
The Last Confederate Tree
has begun to blur and fade

at the bottom of a thousand hope chests.
Now that everything is the past, what use
could a tree have? An old tree,

that no one thought
would die, that was there,
held its arms unfurled over soldiers

as they slept, soldiers unaware
their world would soon die, but not
the tree shading them, not the shade.

EXHIBITION IN THE MUSEUM OF DAYS

Put the days behind glass
and hold them there forever, this one
brought into relief
by drought and heat,
enters the museum as the hottest
and driest day of all time, even more
than 31 years ago, which was
the record. I was 5. The events
that would lead to the Brady Bill
were recorded inadvertently.
We imagine an angel with a quill pen
gazing out the window at all of history, but here
it's Norm the Weatherman saying
we did it, beat the record going
back to 1981. News ratings are up,
everyone watching to see
how famous the day was.
Norm is keeping track.
By the end of August
everything is broken—most days
over 100, longest streak without rain,
hottest ever. Days that will live forever
in the hall of days. When people meet our son
they say to us *you got so lucky.*
Here, in historic drought,
signs in front of churches say
Pray for rain. Do we ask
the clouds? We prayed
for a baby, which means we asked
that someone would get pregnant
and feel overwhelmed, would find
our agency, our name.

WE ARE HAPPY

We are driving to meet the mother
of our son, to meet our son, we are happy.
It takes years to do this. I-10 is a thread
between two cities and we move
along that thread, towards her,
towards him, through fields
and prairies, have dinner
and show photos
of our lives. We come back—
the thread seems precarious,
one end could easily let go.
We don't touch her stomach
at this meeting: it is
her stomach, her baby.
He's there with us,
folded up beneath water
and flesh. She keeps him warm,
knows his habits, forgot to bring
the sonogram. Ten hour round trip
and she decided yes, and we
decided yes. At 18, this will be the hardest thing
she's ever had to do. And for as long as she lives.
I'll call you with my first contractions.
It takes years
to do this, takes our bodies
failing us, all the known science
must fail us, it takes
birth control failing her. It takes years.
They are wonderful years.
It will be pain
and it will be joy. We will be sad
and we will be happy.

NOTES

We Are Happy: The exhibition *Your Bright Future: 12 Contemporary Artists from Korea* at the Museum of Fine Arts, Houston (November, 2009—February 2010) included the artist Bahc Yiso, whose enormous orange billboards hung throughout the city with the single phrase "We Are Happy" in Korean.

Ghazal: The image of a love poem locked in a chest at the bottom of the sea is from Stephen Dunn's "Homage to the Divers."

A Current Atlas of the Commonwealth of Virginia: epigraph from Seferis, "Thrush," Keely and Sherrard translation.

We Will Never Forget: During October 2002, the "D.C. Sniper" terrorized areas around Washington D.C. and along Interstate 95, canvassing as far south as Richmond, Virginia. For the entire time of the killings, people were told the shootings were coming from a white van, which was never true.

In the Conservation Room: A Bruker Artax Spectrometer is an x-ray that allows art conservators to learn about pigments and materials of a painting or sculpture, without the need to physically touch it and thereby degrade its quality or damage it in any way.

Ode: To the People Who Drive By and Shout Insults While I'm Jogging: The final two stanzas of the poem adapt language and images from various *Odes* by Horace, translated by David Ferry.

Case Assessment: Epigraph from Rilke, *The Sonnets to Orpheus*, 1.12, Poulin translation.

Recurring Dream of the Museum: The Jade Hand: Hand-Shaped Pendant, Olmec, 500 B.C., collection of the Museum of Fine Arts, Houston

The National Museum of Funeral History is located in the outskirts of Houston, Texas. A special exhibition on presidential funerals contains the original wire filament from the eternal flame at John F. Kennedy's gravesite in Arlington National Cemetery.

The Last Confederate Tree Tells All: "Now that everything is the past" is a variation on a line from Cavafy's "Remember, Body..."

ACKNOWLEDGMENTS

Carolina Quarterly: "Stargazer's Field"

Copper Nickel: "The Last Confederate Tree Tells All"

Cream City Review: "Case Assessment"

Cutbank: "At the Museum of Funeral History" and "Unpacking the Stone Buddha"

Green Mountains Review online: "We Will Never Forget" and "Talking it Out Before Category 4"

North American Review: "In the Conservation Room"

Nimrod: "Ghazal"

Passages North: "Preservation"

Prairie Schooner: "Braids"

Quarterly West: "In the Museum of Personal History" and "We Are Happy (We are driving to meet the mother of our son...)"

Southern Humanities Review: "Ode: To the People Who Drive By and Shout Insults while I'm Jogging"

42 *Opus*: "Late Shift in the Children's Section" (as "A Brilliant Flash of Light")

"Unpacking the Stone Buddha" was reprinted in the *Cutbank* 40th *Anniversary Anthology*.

"Exhibition in the Museum of Days" appeared at the *Carolina Quarterly/CQ Online* website as part of a Pushcart Prize nomination feature.

I am grateful and indebted to many who have supported me and the work throughout the years: Susan Williams, Patty Paine, Kathy Davis, Peter B. Hyland, Lauren Berry, Brandon Lamson, Glenn Shaheen, Hayan Charara, Nikky Finney, Greg Donovan, David Wojahn, Tony Hoagland, Jeff Lodge, J. Kastely, and Mary Flinn.

The first draft of this book was completed at the Vermont Studio Center with the support of an artist's residency fellowship. Thank you: Nubil Kayshap, Sam Taylor, Tara, Jill, Zelda, and Gary. Thank you to Amy Purvis and the Museum of Fine Arts, Houston, for work and for leave.

For friendship and support, my love to the Harris fam: Paul, Erica, Maggie and Henry.

The interior text and display type were set in Adobe Jenson, a faithful electronic version of the 1470 roman face of Nicolas Jenson. Jenson was a Frenchman employed as the mintmaster at Tours. Legend has it that he was sent to Mainz in 1458 by Charles VII to learn the new art of printing in the shop of Gutenberg, and import it to France. But he never returned, appearing in Venice in 1468; there his first roman types appeared, in his edition of Eusebius. He moved to Rome at the invitation of Pope Sixtus IV, where he died in 1480.

Type historian Daniel Berkeley Updike praises the Jenson Roman for "its readability, its mellowness of form, and the evenness of color in mass." Updike concludes, "Jenson's roman types have been the accepted models for roman letters ever since he made them, and, repeatedly copied in our own day, have never been equalled."

The title on the front and back cover was set in Franklin Gothic. Morris Fuller Benton created the original version in 1902. It is a timeless addition to every font collection, and its applications are innumerable. The design is clean and easily legible and its weight strikes a balanced harmony, making it perfect for both serious and lighthearted content, and everything in between. Benton named the font in honor of Benjamin Franklin who was a prolific printer and typesetter. The text on the front and back cover and the author's name were set in Miller. Miller is a serif typeface, designed by Matthew Carter and named for William Miller. The font and its many variants are widely used, mostly in newspapers and magazines.

Silverfish Review Press is committed to preserving ancient forests and natural resources. We elected to print *Natural History* on 30% post consumer recycled paper, processed chlorine free. As a result, for this printing, we have saved: 1 tree (40' tall and 6-8" diameter), 499 gallons of water, 293 kilowatt hours of electricity, 64 pounds of solid waste, and 120 pounds of greenhouse gases. Thomson-Shore, Inc. is a member of Green Press Initiative, a nonprofit program dedicated to supporting authors, publishers, and suppliers in their efforts to reduce their use of fiber obtained from endangered forests. For more information, visit www.greenpressinitiative.org.

Cover design by Valerie Brewster, Scribe Typography
Text design by Rodger Moody and Connie Kudura, ProtoType
Printed on acid-free papers and bound by Thomson-Shore, Inc.